Where's the Water?

PRECIPITATION

By Caitie McAneney

Gareth Stevens
PUBLISHING

Please visit our website, www.garethstevens.com. For a free color catalog of all our high-quality books, call toll free 1-800-542-2595 or fax 1-877-542-2596.

Cataloging-in-Publication Data

Names: McAneney, Caitie.
Title: Precipitation / Caitie McAneney.
Description: New York : Gareth Stevens Publishing, 2017. | Series: Where's the water? | Includes index.
Identifiers: ISBN 9781482446845 (pbk.) | ISBN 9781482446869 (library bound) | ISBN 9781482446852 (6 pack)
Subjects: LCSH: Precipitation (Meteorology)–Juvenile literature. | Rain and rainfall–Juvenile literature. | Snow–Juvenile literature.
Classification: LCC QC924.7 M43 2017| DDC 551.57'7 –dc23

First Edition

Published in 2017 by
Gareth Stevens Publishing
111 East 14th Street, Suite 349
New York, NY 10003

Copyright © 2017 Gareth Stevens Publishing

Designer: Katelyn E. Reynolds
Editor: Kristen Nelson

Photo credits: Cover, p. 1 Adam Gryko/Shutterstock.com; cover, pp. 1–24 (background) vitalez/
Shutterstock.com; pp. 4–21 (circle splash) StudioSmart/Shutterstock.com; p. 5 Kazakova Maryia/
Shutterstock.com; p. 7 Prometheus72/Shutterstock.com; p. 9 Siwabud Veerapaisarn/Shutterstock.com;
p. 10 chris64/Shutterstock.com; p. 11 NINA MOURIER/The Image Bank/Getty Images; p. 13 (inset)
Martin Puddy/The Image Bank/Getty Images; p. 13 (main) Wesley Bocxe/Science Source/Getty
Images; p. 15 Rashid Valitov/Shutterstock.com; p. 17 Dan Sedran/Shutterstock.com; p. 19 John
Normile/Getty Images; p. 20 Rena Schild/Shutterstock.com; p. 21 David L. Ryan/The Boston Globe
via Getty Images.

Printed in the United States of America

CPSIA compliance information: Batch #CS16GS : For further information contact Gareth Stevens, New York, New York at 1-800-542-2595.

CONTENTS

Words in the glossary appear in **bold** type the first time they are used in the text.

WHAT IS PRECIPITATION?

Imagine you're playing outside when you notice a big, gray cloud overhead. It's just a matter of time before the precipitation starts. It's time to run inside!

Precipitation is water that falls to the ground. It's an important part of the **water cycle**. Water exists on Earth in oceans, lakes, streams, and groundwater. Some water evaporates, or turns into vapor, and floats up to the sky. When this vapor condenses, or changes back to a liquid, that makes precipitation.

Facts on Tap

Most precipitation happens as rain or snow.

This picture of the water cycle shows how water moves from Earth's surface, into the **atmosphere**, and returns to Earth. The water cycle affects weather patterns in our world.

CONDENSATION

PRECIPITATION

SNOW

RAIN

EVAPORATION

SURFACE RUNOFF

GROUNDWATER

WE NEED PRECIPITATION

What if there were no precipitation on Earth? We wouldn't be able to live here! All living things need some amount of water in order to live and grow.

Plants need rain to make their food. People and animals need to eat plants and drink water. The whole **food chain** depends on water. Many living things live in **temperate** and **tropical** areas that get a lot of rain, such as rainforests. Some places, like deserts, get little precipitation, and fewer living things can survive there.

Facts on Tap

Without precipitation, there would be no groundwater for us to use. Groundwater is the water underground people use for wells, watering crops, and more.

Water shortage is a major problem for people living in and near deserts. When there's a long period of time with much less precipitation than usual or no precipitation, it's called a drought.

WHAT IS WATER VAPOR?

Water is in the air around us. Humidity is the amount of water vapor in the air. The more humid it is, the more water vapor is in the air.

When water vapor comes together, it forms fog if it's near the ground or a cloud if it's in the sky. Fog and clouds are filled with tiny drops of water called droplets. Sometimes droplets come together and form heavier drops. When they're heavy enough, the drops fall to earth as a liquid (rain) or solid (snow).

facts on Tap

Have you ever walked through fog? Fog is just a cloud that's near the ground. The air is thick with water vapor.

8

Some places, like rainforests, are very humid.

9

RAIN, RAIN, GO AWAY!

Most people would rather have a sunny day than a rainy day. However, we need rain! Rain happens when water vapor condenses into liquid drops heavy enough to fall.

Not all rain is the same. When it drizzles, tiny droplets of rain fall from the sky. You might barely feel them at all. Other times, the drops are larger. You might get really wet! This is called a rain shower. Rain showers can last just a few minutes, or sometimes it rains all day.

It can even rain when it's sunny out!

EXTREME RAIN

Extreme rain can cause flooding, harm buildings and crops, and even kill people. Extreme rain often happens as part of a hurricane—a swirling tropical storm. In just 1 day, a hurricane can drop more than 2.4 trillion gallons (9 trillion L) of rain, made worse by high winds.

Each summer in Southeast Asia, there's extreme rain brought on by a monsoon. A monsoon is a seasonal change in wind direction. The heavy rainfall floods towns and cities each year and can cause dangerous mudslides.

facts on Tap

People in Southeast Asia depend on the rainfall from the summer monsoons to water their crops. They also use the rushing water to produce electricity.

Millions of people lost their homes and more than 1,800 people died as a result of Hurricane Katrina in August 2005. Eighty percent of New Orleans, Louisiana, was flooded for weeks after.

monsoon

13

IT'S COLD OUT!

Sometimes it's too cold for rain and too warm for snow. Then, you might see a mix of snow, ice, and rain.

Sleet is a mixture of snow and rain. It's more like freezing slush than snow. Hail occurs when ice crystals move up and down inside a cloud, adding a new coating of ice each time they jump high into the clouds. They finally get so heavy they drop to earth. Hail can cause a lot of **damage**.

facts on Tap

Some hail chunks can be as large as baseballs. The largest ever was about the size of a volleyball!

Sometimes rain freezes once it hits a surface, such as the road or a car. This is called freezing rain, or glaze.

LET IT SNOW!

When the temperature reaches 32°F (0°C), water vapor forms a solid—snow. Russia, Greenland, Canada, and the northern United States have snow every year. Tiny pieces of dirt or other matter combine with water droplets in the air. Ice crystals form around them to make snow! When snowflakes become heavy enough, they fall to the ground.

Some snowflakes are small and light, while others are big and fluffy. Many melt when they hit the ground. However, if the ground is cold enough, snow can start to pile up.

Facts on Tap

Some snow falls as hard, small balls called graupel (GROU-puhl).

16

A snowflake can be made of up to 200 ice crystals!

TONS OF SNOW

When a lot of snow falls in a short amount of time, there can be trouble. Small flakes can soon pile up into feet of snow. Streets can be covered in snow, making it hard to drive. People can be trapped in their homes. Snow can weigh down power lines, causing them to snap, which leaves people without electricity.

Lake-effect snowstorms and nor'easters are big storms that happen as wind moves over lakes and oceans. This causes water to evaporate and form big clouds that can drop a lot of precipitation.

Facts on Tap

The Iran Blizzard of 1972 is the deadliest blizzard in history. More than 26 feet (8 m) of snow fell on 200 villages, burying people and buildings. Nearly 4,000 people were killed.

Blizzards are snowstorms with high winds. The winds often create large drifts of snow that can cover cars and even reach the tops of houses.

19

CHANGING WEATHER

Scientists think the amount and **intensity** of precipitation will change as **global climate change** occurs. Scientists believe climate change is mostly caused by human activities, such as burning **fossil fuels** and cutting down trees.

Global climate change may cause big weather events such as hurricanes and blizzards to happen more often and with more strength. It can also cause droughts, making it hard to live in dry areas. It's important that we treat our Earth with respect and be thankful for precipitation!

Many people speak out against the use of fossil fuels because of the part they play in global climate change.

Deadly Precipitation

1888: Schoolhouse Blizzard of 1888 – Minnesota – at least 235 deaths

1900: Great Galveston Hurricane – Galveston, Texas – 6,000-8,000 deaths

1972: Blizzard of 1972 – Iran – 4,000 deaths

1997: Hurricane Pauline – Mexico – 230 to 500 deaths

2005: Hurricane Katrina – Louisiana, Alabama, Mississippi, Georgia, Florida – 1,800 deaths

2012: Hurricane Sandy – Caribbean and East Coast of the United States – 285 deaths

Hurricane Sandy

GLOSSARY

atmosphere: the mixture of gases that surrounds a planet

damage: harm

extreme: very great

food chain: a line of living things, each of which uses the one before it for food

fossil fuel: matter formed over millions of years from plant and animal remains that's burned for power

global climate change: long-term change in Earth's weather, caused partly by human activities such as burning oil and natural gas

intensity: amount of strength or force

temperate: mild weather that's not too hot or too cold

tropical: having to do with the warm parts of Earth near the equator

water cycle: the series of conditions through which water passes from vapor in the air to liquid or solid falling on Earth's surface and finally rising back into the air

FOR MORE INFORMATION

Books

Johnson, Robin. *What Is Precipitation?* St. Catharines, Ontario, Canada: Crabtree Publishing, 2013.

Rao, Joe. *The Cool Story Behind Snow.* New York, NY: Simon Spotlight, 2015.

Websites

Moisture in the Atmosphere
www.kidsgeo.com/geography-for-kids/0100-atmospheric-moisture.php
Use the links on the left of this site to explore different kinds of precipitation!

Precipitation: The Water Cycle
water.usgs.gov/edu/watercycleprecipitation.html
Learn more about how raindrops form and which areas of the world get the most precipitation.

The Water Cycle
pmm.nasa.gov/education/water-cycle
Get an up-close look at the water cycle from NASA!

INDEX